to my dad
who
always gently
encourages
creative perfection.
-kz

First Published 2000 by:
Dimensional Illustrators, Inc.
For HBI, an imprint of
HarperCollins Publishers
10 East 53rd Street
New York, NY 10022-5299 USA
ISBN: 0688-17993-2

Distributed in the U.S. and Canada by:
Watson-Guptill Publications
1515 Broadway
New York, NY 10036 USA
800-451-1741 Telephone
732-363-4511 Telephone in NJ, AK, HI
732-363-0338 Fax
ISBN: 0-8230-7408-0

Distributed throughout the rest of the world by:
HarperCollins International
10 East 53rd Street
New York, NY 10022-5299 USA
212-207-7654 Fax

First Published in Germany by:
NIPPAN

Nippon Shuppan Hanbai
Deutschland GmbH
Krefelder Strasse 85
D-40549 Dusseldorf
0211-5048080 Telephone
0211-5049326 Fax
ISBN: 3-931884-69-4

© Copyright 2000 by Dimensional Illustrators, Inc. and HBI, an imprint of HarperCollins Publishers

Address Direct Mail Sales to:
Dimensional Illustrators, Inc.
362 Second Street Pike / Suite 112
Southampton, PA 18966 USA
215-953-1415 Telephone
215-953-1697 Fax
Email: dimension@3dimillus.com
Website: http://www.3dimillus.com

Printed in Hong Kong

All rights reserved. No part of this book may be used or reproduced in any form or by an electronic or mechanical means, including information storage and retrieval systems, without written permission of the copyright owners, except by a reviewer who may quote brief passages in a review. The captions, information and artwork in this book have been supplied by the designers and illustrators. All works have been reproduced on the condition they are reproduced with the knowledge and prior consent of the designers, clients, companies and/or other interested parties. No responsibility is accepted by Dimensional Illustrators, Inc.; HBI, an imprint of HarperCollins Publishers, or printer for any infringement of copyright or otherwise arising from the contents of this publication. Every effort has been made to ensure captions accurately comply with information supplied. The publisher cannot under any circumstances accept responsibility for errors or omissions. All products or name brands used in this book are trademarks registered trademarks or tradenames of their respective holders.

pixel perfect

edited by
Kathleen Ziegler and Nick Greco

Watson-Guptill

HBI
an imprint of HarperCollins International

pixelperfect credits

Creative Director / Associate Editor
Kathleen Ziegler / Dimensional Illustrators, Inc.

Executive Editor
Nick Greco / Dimensional Illustrators, Inc.

Book Design, Jacket Cover Design & Typography
Deborah Davis / Davis Design

Copywriter
Cathy Fishel / Catharine & Sons

Cover Art
Stuart Bradford ©Copyright 2000

Adobe Photoshop, Dimensions, Illustrator, Streamline, Fontstudio and Premiere are registered trademarks of Adobe Systems Incorporated. Fractal Design Painter and Infini-D are registered trademarks of MetaCreations Corporation. Shima Seiki is a registered trademark product of Shima Seiki. Macromedia Director, Freehand, Flash, Fireworks, Dreamweaver and Sound Edit are registered trademarks of Macromedia Corporation. BBedit is a registered product of Bare Bones Software, Inc. GrooveMaker is a registered trademark property of IK Multimedia Production. Softimage is a registered trademark of Avid Technology or its subsidiaries or divisions. Apple Video Player is a registered trademark product of Apple Computer, Inc. All other brand or product names used in this book are trademarks, registered trademarks or trademarks of their respective holders.

KELLY LIBRARY
EMORY & HENRY COLLEGE
EMORY, VA 24327

contents

introduction 8

advertising 10
Advertisements, Advertising Campaigns, Brochure Mailers, Licensing Images, Posters, Sell Tags, Logo Designs

editorial 42
Art for Charity, Booklets, Brochures, Editorials, Font Creation, Greeting Cards, Illustrations, Magazine Covers, Poetic Illustrations

websites 88
Ezines, Gallery Websites, Homepages, Online Design Exhibitions, Websites, Web Screen Designs

books, calendars, music media 110
Book Covers, Book Illustrations, Calendars, Compact Disc Covers, CD Disc Packaging, CD Rom Packaging

exploratory 132
Experimental, Fine Art, Personal Work, Promotional Posters, Self-Promotional

directory of artists 156

8

introduction

PixelPerfect reveals what happens when the truly adventurous artistic spirit meets new media. Thirty-one digital creatives from the United States, Brazil, Italy and New Zealand, renown for the relentless pursuit of their imaginations, share the success stories and symbolism behind each inspired illustration. They surpass the norm in each assignment, using powerful creativity and computers to seize our attention and influence the way we view advertising and publishing media.

The potency of digitally generated art: This is the cornerstone of **PixelPerfect**'s philosophy. The book's chapters include Advertising; Editorial; Books, Calendars, Music Media; Websites; plus an extraordinary bonus section on Exploratory work.

This collection of digital creativity offers fresh insights as it generates inspiration. Few publications permit you to decipher the chaotic imagery of the artistic imagination like **PixelPerfect**.

– Kathleen Ziegler and Nick Greco
Dimensional Illustrators, Inc.

advertising

pixel perfect

PROMO SPREAD 2 digital creator JEFF BRICE client JEFF BRICE software ADOBE PHOTOSHOP, FREEHAND, METACREATIONS INFINI-D purpose POSTER
Jeff Brice's self-promotion poster celebrates the millennium with positive imagery, while working to dissuade any negative attitudes. The focus of the illustration and text is remapping, recoding and redefining ourselves in a more positive fashion, a process of flight and navigation of imagination which he calls the "New Cartography".

PROMO SPREAD 1 digital creator JEFF BRICE client JEFF BRICE software ADOBE PHOTOSHOP, FREEHAND, METACREATIONS INFINI-D purpose POSTER

Artist Jeff Brice wanted to prevent any negative perceptions that have emerged for the millennium when he created this self-promotional poster, titled "New Cartographies." Brice emphasizes the way in which we map our world, our bodies and our perceptions. He acknowledges that the 21st century may require us to find alternative ways of thinking and recharting our paths, but the symbolism and wayfaring will remain comfortably familiar. *Hand Photo Courtesy of PhotoDisc

FACE, EL DIABLITO, PEAR AND HAND digital creator WALTER ROBERTSON software ADOBE PHOTOSHOP, METACREATIONS PAINTER purpose LICENSING IMAGES

"Eye candy" – this was Walter Robertson's goal in creating a series of illustrations he could license and market to Gen-Xers for reproduction on such products as mouse pads, stationery, clothing and in advertising. In his bright, bold, graphic images, Robertson plays off of art on old Mexican lottery cards, building on their symbolic references. The result is art that is unlike other imagery on the market.

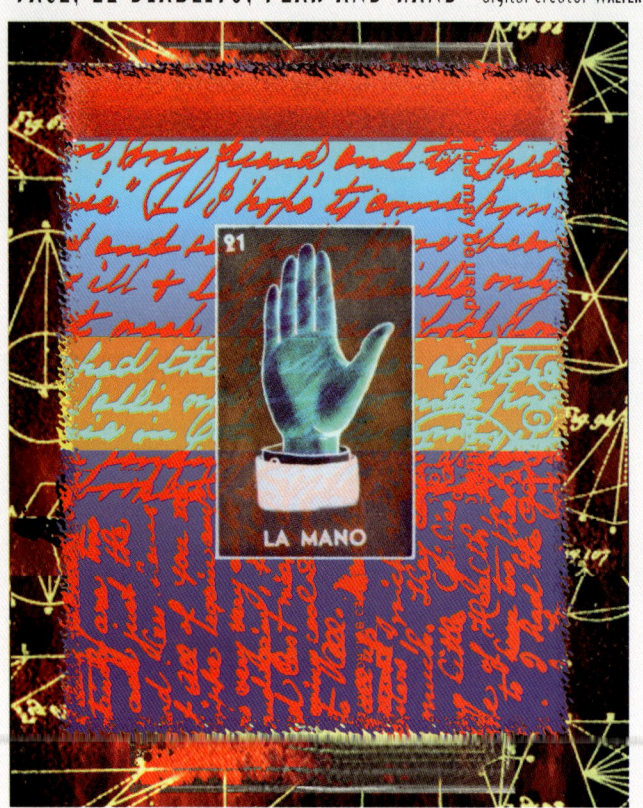

LIMN GALLERY POSTER digital creator **JONATHAN CAPONI** client **LIMN GALLERY** software **ADOBE ILLUSTRATOR, ADOBE PHOTOSHOP** purpose **POSTER**

Jonathan Caponi represents the rage to survive in this poster titled "Animals: The Extinct to the Improbable," which he created for an exhibition at Limn Gallery. To demonstrate graphically the losing game animals play against humans, Caponi illustrated claw marks on a bloody background. The marks were then made more realistic with diecutting. It's as if a desperate beast has slashed the paper to shreds.

POSTER SERIES digital creators **IGORS IRBE, INGUNA IRBE** client **IRBE DESIGN** software **ADOBE PHOTOSHOP, ADOBE DIMENSIONS, QUARKXPRESS** purpose **SELF-PROMOTION POSTERS**

This series of three mini posters was created by Igors Irbe of Irbe Design over a two year period. The artist pulled out an array of common and intriguing elements from his library of visual images. The finished posters are metaphors of everyday objects, he explains. Everyday life is all about repetition: In fact, it adds structure and a sort of comforting balance. At the same time, degradation and a touch of chaos provides interest.

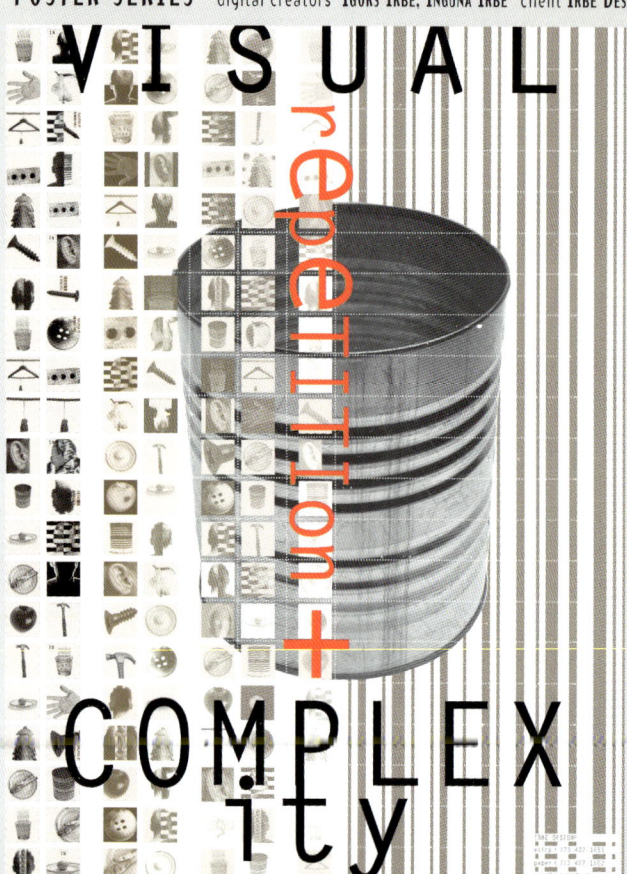

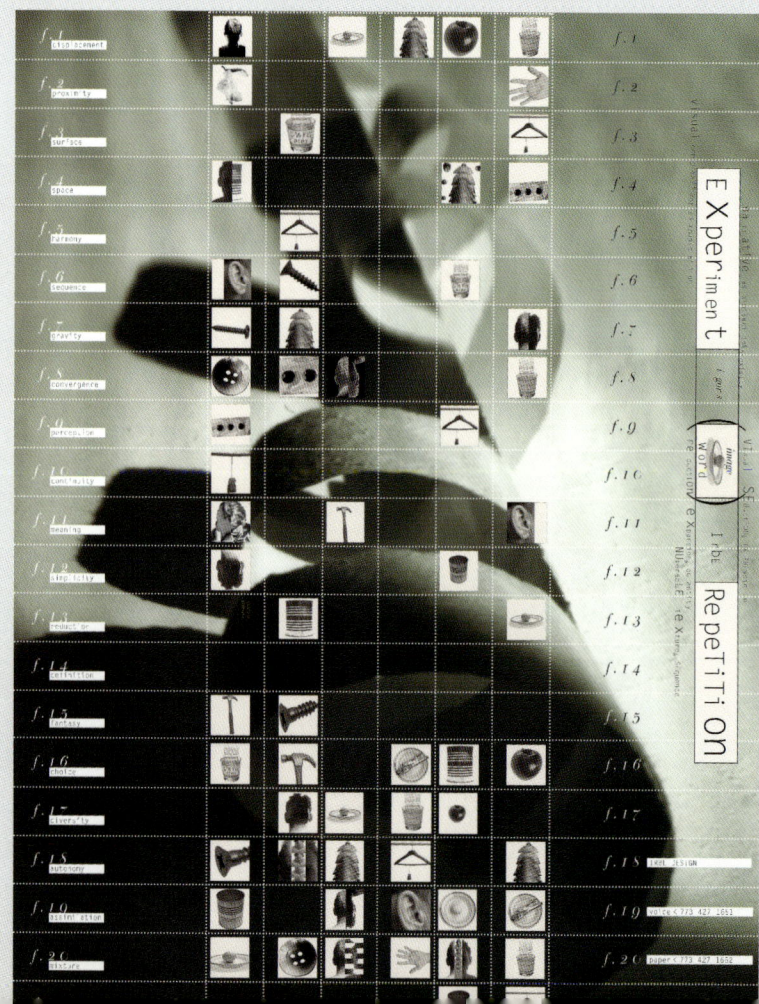

DOMINION digital creator **RUSSELL MANN** client **DOMINION NIGHTCLUB** software **ADOBE PHOTOSHOP, ADOBE ILLUSTRATOR** purpose **PROMOTIONAL POSTER**
The owner of the Dominion night club wanted to attract a wider audience. He did not want a poster that looked gothic, like his previous posters. Artist Russell Mann's solution was to use more color and contrast, and keep the use of black to a minimum. He also wanted to project a subtle feeling of decay and corrosion. To accomplish this, he used decomposing diagonal lines in the background and a moth in the lower left corner to establish an organic yet dynamic feel.

RUSH INTO THE UNKNOWN   digital creator **BILL KOEB**   client **KATSIN/LOEB ADVERTISING**   software **ADOBE PHOTOSHOP**   purpose **ADVERTISING CAMPAIGN**

This is the first in a series of images that Bill Koeb illustrated for the current Fireman's Fund advertising campaign. Allison Burton, art director at Katsin/Loeb Advertising, wanted an image about feeling secure enough with your insurance carrier to take risks, and resonate with the copy: "Life is a rush into the unknown". After discussing many possibilities, including the cliché of a man walking down a road, Koeb created this image of a man flying fearlessly into the unknown, feeling safe enough to take any risk, face any future.

SHOOT ME digital creator **MARK ALLEN** client **GOLDSTROM GALLERY** software **QuarkXPress, Adobe Photoshop** purpose **POSTER**

To announce an exhibit of vintage and contemporary photography in which his own work would be featured, Mark Allen designed this remarkable postcard. Allen thought it would be interesting to show an image he snapped on the street in Washington, D.C. It is a picture of a photograph of Marilyn Monroe with bits and pieces torn off and graffiti scribbled on top. "It is an image in a state of wonderful decay," says the artist. Images from previous posters show through the tears, which he thought was a perfect way of juxtaposing the vintage with the contemporary.

CUBANITO digital creator **CRISTINA CASAÑAS** client **LATIN POETRY WEEK** software **ADOBE PHOTOSHOP** purpose **ILLUSTRATION**

Cubanito, created for "Latin Poetry in a Week," this Cristina Casañas illustration resembles a very old poster, peeling from paint-chipped walls of colonial Havana. The artist superimposed the words and image of the famous Cuban poet, José Martí, over the work. Martí inspired revolution with his writing; today, he is a symbol for freedom fighters throughout the world. The cool blue and green colors, together with glimpses of latino architecture and the landscape, portray the struggle that is very personal to the author and his culture.

APHRODISIAC SELL TAG digital creator DESIGNAHOLIX client APHRODISIAC CLOTHING AND ACCESSORIES software ADOBE PHOTOSHOP purpose SELL TAG FOR CLOTHING AND ACCESSORIES

Aphrodisiac, a clothing and accessory brand, wanted to appeal personally to its consumers with the products they sell. To achieve their goal, the Jenson brothers of Designaholix used warm earth tones combined with progressive digital surrealism. The Jensons feel that so much digital design uses cold, rigid aesthetics to communicate "technology." The earth tones and painted face, support a warmer, organic relationship between humanity and electronic media.

DIGITANGO LOGO digital creator LEE LAND client DIGITANGO software SHIMA SEIKI purpose LOGO

Digitango's company logo was created by Lee Land from an illustrator file of graphics, scans of different textures and various layering techniques. Digitango, is a digital retouching studio, that conquers the most challenging projects, as well as, providing excellence in illustration.

HONDA 2000 BROCHURES digital creator **John Ritter** hand lettering **Lilly Lee** client **Honda** software **Adobe Photoshop** purpose **Brochure Covers**

These images, created by John Ritter, were a radical departure for Honda Motor Company, a normally conservative organization which has historically used straight forward photography in its brochures. For the client's year 2000 automobile brochures, Ritter wanted to create impressionistic imagery that evokes the emotion and personality of each car in a non-literal fashion. His images are rich in color and texture, incorporating calligraphic letterforms by internationally known calligrapher Lilly Lee.

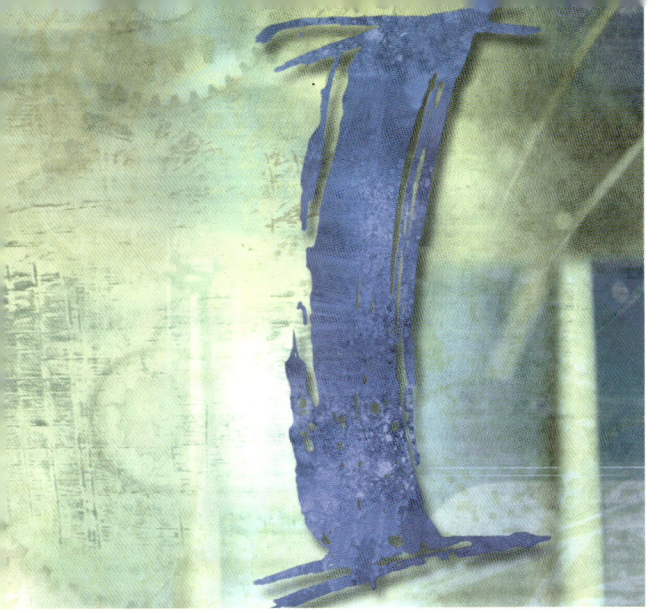

42

pixel perfect

editorial

43

STRING THEORY digital creator **STUART BRADFORD** client **ELECTRONIC MUSICIAN MAGAZINE** software **ADOBE PHOTOSHOP** purpose **EDITORIAL**
To illustrate an article on a technology that allows musicians to produce realistic string sounds with the computer, artist Stuart Bradford played off the concept of "plugging in" to anything new. He didn't want anything that would be considered conventionally high-tech, so his image for the Electronic Musician Magazine piece includes classic profiles of violins merged with electrical outlets; below are plugs emerging from vintage photos of keyboards and pianists, just waiting to be synthesized.

GENDER CONFUSION digital creator STUART BRADFORD client UTNE READER MAGAZINE software ADOBE PHOTOSHOP purpose EDITORIAL

Getting to know others and ourselves has taken on an entirely new and sometimes strange face on the internet. Created by Stuart Bradford for an Utne Reader article on online chat rooms that cater to those who toy with their true identities, these illustrations play with both real and conceptual reflection and magnification. This interpretation was a bold departure from his usual work and a rare glimpse into his ability to push the imagination of those who wonder who their inner personalities might be.

SEX ADDICT digital creator HENRIK DRESCHER client D.J. STOUT, TEXAS MONTHLY software ADOBE PHOTOSHOP purpose EDITORIAL

Texas Monthly magazine commissioned Henrik Drescher for an editorial illustration on the hot topic of sexual addiction. Since Drescher already had sexual-oriented characters populating some of his notebooks, he skipped the sketch phase and moved directly to the final rendering. The image of the woman on the left is pasted all over with sexual innuendoes while the man, with a brain the size of a pea, hangs his personality on his manhood. His preferences preface even his personality.

ANIMAL SPIRIT digital creative MICHAEL MORGENSTERN client MICHAEL MORGENSTERN software ADOBE PHOTOSHOP purpose PERSONAL PIECE

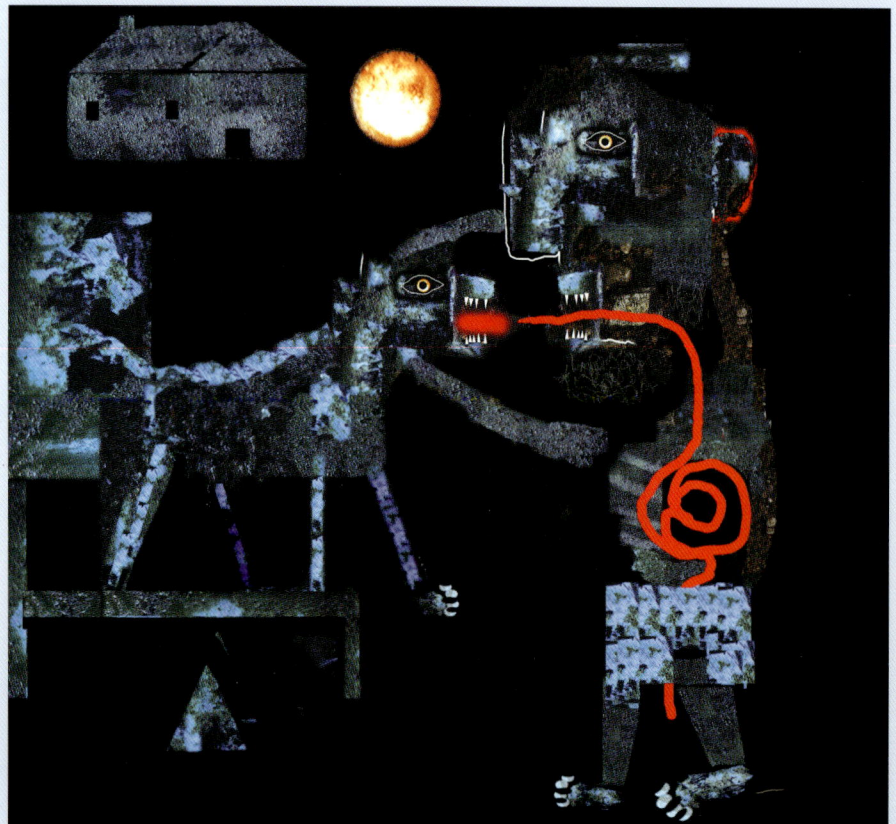

Inspired by Herman Hesse's Steppenwolf, Michael Morgenstern created this personal work to explore Freud's concept of the id. The artist gave parts of the same face with sharp teeth to both the man and animal, to depict the presence of instinctual behaviors and appetites in both creatures. The scene takes place in the unconscious of night, outside the home, where we tend to view ourselves in a more civil light.

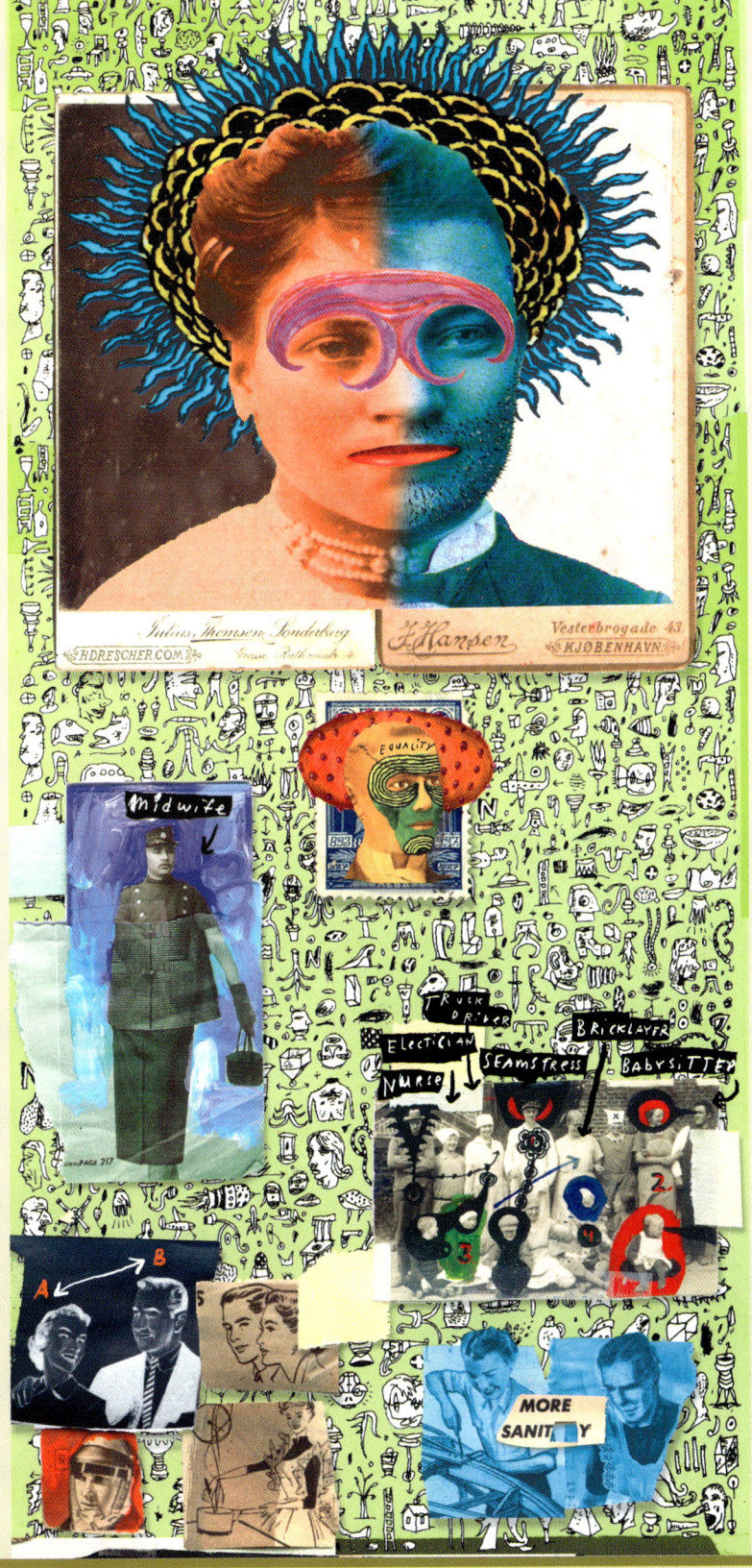

EQUAL RIGHTS digital creator Henrik Drescher client HK Union, Denmark software Adobe Photoshop purpose Information Booklet

HK Union, a trade union in Denmark, asked Henrik Drescher to create an illustration for its information booklet that dealt with sexual equality in the work place. Drescher's solution was to create gender confusion. The central portrait image is androgynous, pearls on one side of the neck and a collar on the other; a woman's hairstyle on one side and a man's on the other. A blazing crown unites the pieces into one symbolic figure. More snippets of male/female dichotomy float below, together with what he calls "image drape," a wonderfully involved inventory of drawings from Drescher's notebooks.

LUNCH WITH CHER digital creator **Tom Nick Cocotos** client **Miami Metro Magazine** software **Adobe Photoshop** purpose **Editorial**

Tom Nick Cocotos produced this Modigliani-style portrait of Cher for Miami Metro Magazine's "Salsa" column. Cher had been a guest on a local radio station's lunch time show, during which she and the host actually ate with the audience. In his typically humorous style, Cocotos contrasts the glamorous diva with the mundane, surrounding her with a sandwich, pickles and olives.

ROSIE O'DONNELL digital creator **Tom Nick Cocotos** client **Miami Metro Magazine** software **Adobe Photoshop** purpose **Editorial**

Tom Nick Cocotos composed this biting portrait of the beloved Rosie O'Donnell for Miami Metro Magazine's "Salsa" column. Here O'Donnell is simple and graphic, simultaneously smiling and a bit sinister. Faux-framing her in a gilt surround instead of her usual television set frame is a sly reference to the star's rather large ego.

TYSON BECKFORD   digital creator TOM NICK COCOTOS   client MIAMI METRO MAGAZINE   software ADOBE PHOTOSHOP   purpose EDITORIAL

For Miami Metro Magazine's monthly celebrity buzz column, "Salsa," artist Tom Nick Cocotos built a discordant but strangely beautiful illustration of super-model Tyson Beckford. A patchwork of shades and flashes portray a young man in the context of admiration. His shirt is only a pencil sketch, representative of how Beckford turns fashion ideas into the hottest-selling styles.

GATES DEVIL   digital creator **GORDON STUDER**   client **MACWORLD MAGAZINE**   software **ADOBE PHOTOSHOP**   purpose **EDITORIAL**

This irreverent editorial illustration was created by Gordon Studer for Macworld magazine for an article titled, "The Dark Side of the Dark Side." The story equated Bill Gates with true evil, which for some isn't a real stretch. The art director wanted to show Gates using manipulative tactics and committing criminal activity in his quest for world domination. This was definitely a devilish Gates. Studer's solution followed this direction literally. He holds the world in his command.

CONVERGENCE   digital creator **GORDON STUDER**   client **FORBESASAP**   software **ADOBE PHOTOSHOP**   purpose **EDITORIAL**

"Coming Distractions: Soon we'll have a new way to get in touch with our innerselves," was the title of a ForbesASAP special section. Written by movie critic, Roger Ebert, the article discussed the convergence of technology and the human body. Embedded computer chips could ultimately create semi-bionic humans who are under a whole new type of control. Illustrator Gordon Studer built a person from computer parts in his typically abstract style. The man's basic form is recognizable as human, but he has definitely been shaped by technology.

ABSTRACT ANGEL digital creator GORDON STUDER client ART FOR AIDS software ADOBE PHOTOSHOP, ADOBE ILLUSTRATOR purpose ART FOR CHARITY

"Abstract Angel" was created by Gordon Studer to promote a charity auction that benefited UCSF AIDS Health Project. The image of an angel was a clear symbolic icon for Studer. He abstracted the figure, breaking it down into color fields and simple shapes. Drawing from Picasso-like palette of colors, he combined elements to form a modern-day figurative icon.

INVESTING TOOLS FOR PERSONAL WEALTH digital creator **Francisco Caceres** client **Bloomberg Personal Finance** software **Adobe Photoshop** purpose **Editorial**
This eye-opening illustration was created by Francisco Caceres as one in a series of editorial pieces for a special section in Bloomberg Personal Finance magazine. The article focused on software from the web that can be used as investing tools in amassing personal wealth. Caceres' approach was to create a hybrid investor—part human and part technology—to show how one can become a master-mind moneymaker.

CEO THREE SPIN, CEO SPIN digital creator LANCE JACKSON client CEO MAGAZINE software APPLE VIDEO PLAYER, ADOBE PHOTOSHOP purpose EDITORIAL
Speed, adaptability, linkages, and cross-overs where competitors become partners and new alliances blossom at unbelievable rates: That's the shape of business today. Lance Jackson created these colorful illustrations for a CEO Magazine article which mused over how fantastic business would be in 2010. Anonymous toy figures in saturated colors stand tall upon spinning tops, above the toiling, work-a-day crowd, shuffling off to their specific jobs. With the benefit of a higher perspective and the speed of their immense organizations, the taller figures continue to spin even faster.

BEST OF SAN FRANCISCO MAGAZINE digital creator FRANCISCO CACERES client SAN FRANCISCO MAGAZINE software ADOBE PHOTOSHOP purpose EDITORIAL

Every year, San Francisco Magazine features a retrospective that highlights local celebrities in its "Best of San Francisco" issue. Francisco Caceres created this image as one in the series, this one spotlighting Jim Clark, the founder of Netscape. Clark's favorite sport of stunt flying is played up in the art, which shows him precariously poised atop a plane. Caceres says the pose shows the navigational risks Clark takes with Netscape.

LOGON digital creator FRANCISCO CACERES client ZD INTERNET PROFESSIONELL software ADOBE PHOTOSHOP purpose EDITORIAL

ZD Internet Professionell is a German publication that commissioned Francisco Caceres to create a spot illustration for a section called, "LogOn." The section features notable people in the news who have uttered some sort of outlandish quote. With all the allegations that Bill Gates must constantly deny, the publication had a quote from a woman at Bloomberg, who said, "If Bill Gates says it's not raining, it's not raining." In his art, Caceres shows a woman with ears like radar dishes. She stretches out her hand in the pouring rain but does not get wet, as long as she is receiving Gates' instructions from the tower.

THE BEAT OF THE CAMPAIGN TRAIL   digital creator FRANCISCO CACERES   client SCHOLASTIC / NEW YORK TIMES UPFRONT   software ADOBE PHOTOSHOP   purpose EDITORIAL

Francisco Caceres' goal in this editorial illustration, for Scholastic/New York Times' magazine Upfront, was to get teenagers interested in what they saw as a boring Presidential primary race. His illustration appeared in Scholastic magazine as well as in the New York Times: Upfront editorial section. Portraying the candidates Gore, Bush and Dole, as rap singers dancing to the beat of their campaign trail, the artist humorously brought the presidential hopefuls into the teen world. Caceres dressed them in the latest cool attire, complete with knit caps and saggy duds.

TEENAGERS AND DNA   digital creator FRANCISCO CACERES   client SCHOLASTIC   software ADOBE PHOTOSHOP   purpose EDITORIAL

DNA genetic studies are discovering more genes that play a crucial role in the appearance of the face and head. Francisco Caceres was asked to create a DNA-scrambled portrait of a teenager for Scholastic Magazine. The art includes a cross-section of facial characteristics from a variety of ethnic backgrounds, representing infinite possibilities. The youthful, genderless face is not as much a Frankenstein character as a positive racial recipe.

55

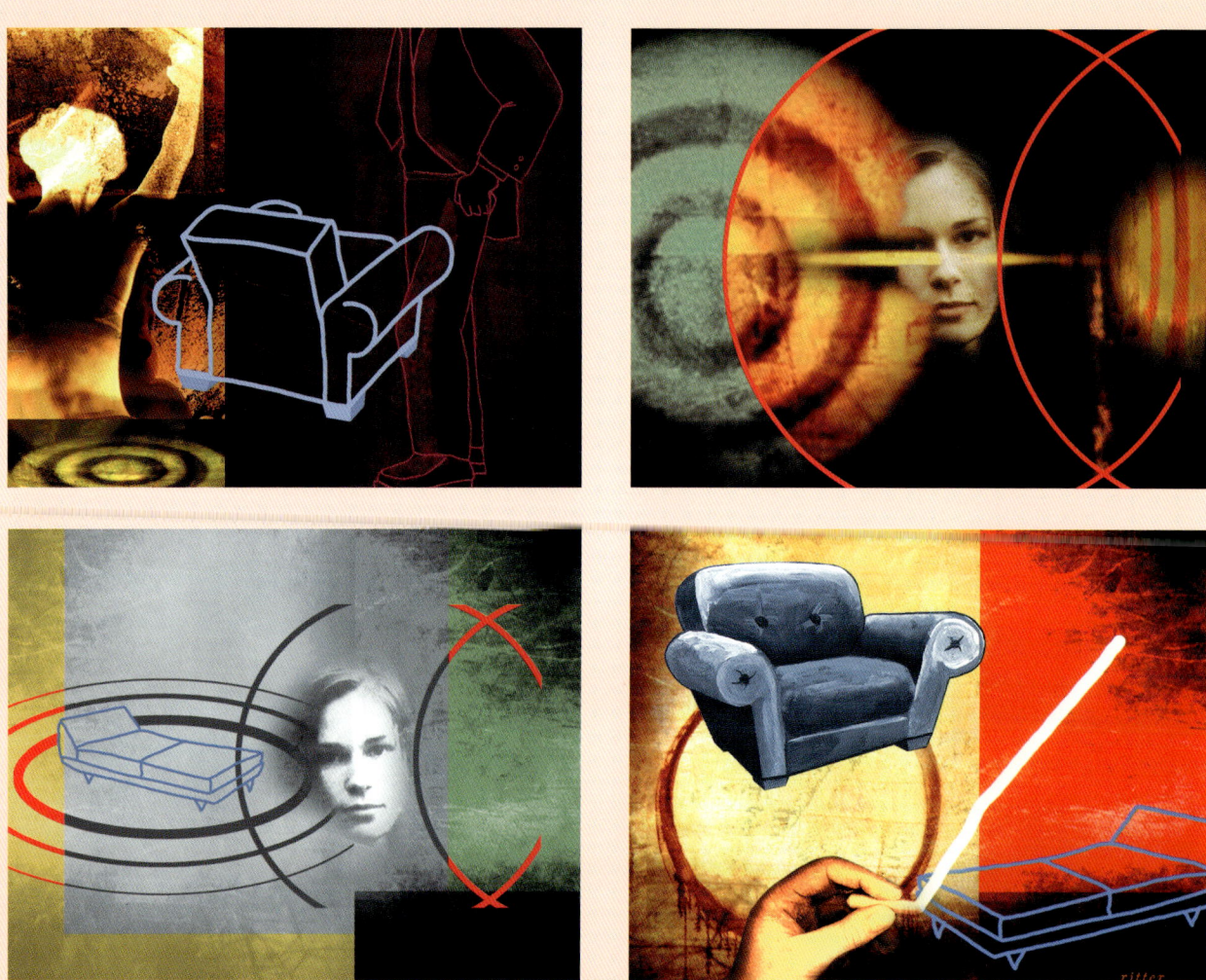

BOUNDARIES   digital creator JOHN RITTER   client PSYCHOLOGY TODAY MAGAZINE   software ADOBE PHOTOSHOP   purpose EDITORIAL

Psychology Today commissioned John Ritter to illustrate a feature article on the boundaries between psychologist and patients. He created four electronic sketches, depicting the various aspects of doctor-patient boundaries. In two images, Ritter explores physical, spatial boundaries of the session: The viewer is placed inside the "room," within the safety zone of the couch. In the other two images, Ritter refers to the emotional barriers that are within the patient. Breaching those boundaries violates the safety of the walls inside the patient's mind. The art director liked the artwork so much that he used them on the cover.

VIDEO MOTEL digital creator STUART BRADFORD client PENTHOUSE LETTERS MAGAZINE software ADOBE PHOTOSHOP purpose EDITORIAL
The discrete world of video motels, where partners videotape themselves under the sheets, is uncovered in this Penthouse editorial illustration rendered by artist Stuart Bradford. By portraying the video camera poised atop sensuous legs, Bradford intimates the unsettling, anonymous nature of the enclosed room.

HEALTHCARE ONLINE digital creator **IGORS IRBE** client **PHYSICIAN'S PRACTICE DIGEST** software **ADOBE PHOTOSHOP** purpose **EDITORIAL COVER**

In this cover for Physician's Practice Digest, Igors Irbe portrays e-companies and their influence on modern technology. The cloned images of the three medical practitioner's are virtual reminders of the generic nature of health care transactions online. Irbe says this is not a picture of the future of health care, but rather what it has become.

MAC HELP CENTER digital creator **KEN ORVIDAS** software **ADOBE PHOTOSHOP** client **MACWORLD** PURPOSE **EDITORIAL**

Macworld needed an image for their magazine and website that would inform Mac users about the offerings of the help center. Many users didn't know the extensive services available to them with just a click. Ken Orvidas created an image that shows a disgruntled computer user who calls out the correct command. The artist used vibrant color and pattern to suggest the energy and possibilities to be found at the site.

TECH FUNDS digital creator ALLEN CRAWFORD client TICKER MAGAZINE software ADOBE PHOTOSHOP purpose EDITORIAL

The tone of a Ticker Magazine article illustrated by Allen Crawford was cautionary: It warned investors with tech funds to keep their eyes open to market trends while diversifying their portfolios. The client wanted the illustration to be relevant, but asked Crawford to pump some life into what could be very dry subject matter. The artist's solution revealed the cautionary character behind the Wall Street business suit as a new breed of investor.

SLAVE TO THE MACHINE digital creator ALLEN CRAWFORD client GETTINGIT.COM software ADOBE PHOTOSHOP purpose EDITORIAL

GettingIt.com is an online magazine well known for being shamefully irreverent. This reputation presented artist Allen Crawford with a great opportunity to create a somewhat eerie image to accompany an article entitled "Slave to the Machine." The story was about a British creative who depends on his computer to come up with ideas for new projects. Crawford's whimsically strange character matched the tone of the text, which questioned the depth to which the computer has invaded even the most human of activities.

BANKRUPTCY digital creator DIANE FENSTER client INC. MAGAZINE software ADOBE PHOTOSHOP purpose EDITORIAL

This poignant portrait of the human face of bankruptcy was composed by Diane Fenster for Inc. Magazine. After researching the different types of fiscal failures on the internet, the artist pulled together one face made from many features. The result is a lost soul-anonymous but sad in a very familiar way. The image was originally a spot illustration in the magazine, but the creative director liked it so much, they ran it as a full page.

MENTORING digital creator SANDY YOUNG client BSSB, CHRISTIAN SINGLE MAGAZINE software ADOBE PHOTOSHOP, ADOBE ILLUSTRATOR purpose MAGAZINE COVER

Sandy Young's client, Christian Single Magazine, supplied stock photographs of the base portrait and marble head that live together in this cover illustration on the subject of "mentoring." Rock surfaces and rough textures, together with the chiseled marble, help to convey the idea that mentoring can be like forming or molding something out of raw materials. The juxtaposition of the two heads suggests both a merging and a separateness of the two figures.

CAMERA DIGITAL digital creator STUART BRADFORD client MACWORLD MAGAZINE software ADOBE PHOTOSHOP purpose EDITORIAL

The more advanced Adobe Photoshop becomes, the more it replicates the goals of traditional photography and darkroom work. Stuart Bradford's objective in this editorial was to illustrate merging the old and new worlds in this software then-and-now for Macworld magazine. The illustration represents the benefits of Photoshop's varied capabilities, whose very advantages the artist utilized to make the image.

CRUNCHING NUMBERS digital creator STUART BRADFORD client PROFILES MAGAZINE software ADOBE PHOTOSHOP purpose EDITORIAL

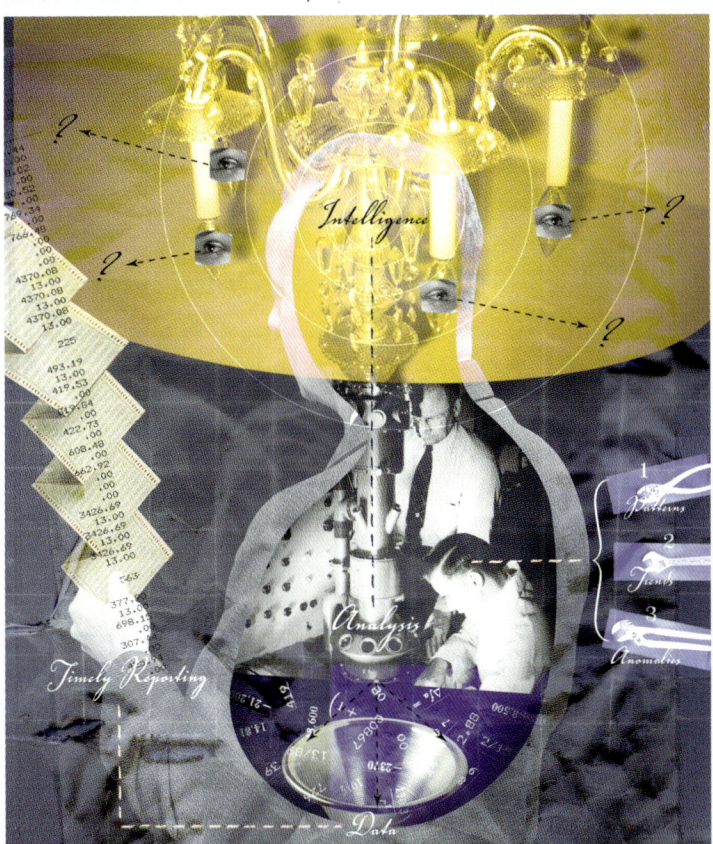

The database manipulation in all its glorious guises is depicted in this editorial illustration for Profiles Magazine, rendered by Stuart Bradford. Numbers are literally crunched, analyzed over and over in the pursuit of corporate truth. As analytical eyes peer down from the inverted chandelier, Bradford focuses on the hidden truth behind the real information.

BO DIDLEY digital creator LANCE JACKSON client SAN FRANCISCO EXAMINER software ADOBE PHOTOSHOP purpose EDITORIAL

You can almost hear the unique blues rock voice of musician Bo Didley in this editorial illustration for the San Francisco Examiner Magazine, created by artist Lance Jackson. His colorful portrait captures the legendary figure with his characteristic black hat and squared-off guitar, but saturates him with cool blues colors. Pixilated areas and agitated hues transmit the energy of Didley's amazing guitar riffs and vocals.

DAVID BOWIE digital creator TOM NICK COCOTOS client BLOOMBERG MAGAZINE software ADOBE PHOTOSHOP purpose EDITORIAL

Tom Nick Cocotos created this illustration of David Bowie - one of his favorite musicians - for a story in Bloomberg Magazine about Asset-Backed Securities. ABSs allow you to invest in a variety of commodities, including performers like Bowie. The graph paper background serves as a subtle financial tie-in to the article's subject matter; the microphone cord provides the fever line representing accelerating stock.

HELL digital creator **HENRIK DRESCHER** client **U.S. NEWS AND WORLD REPORT** software **ADOBE PHOTOSHOP** purpose **EDITORIAL**
This picture, one of a series, began as an idea in Henrik Drescher's sketchbook. The image was drawn from an anthropological photo of an African tribesman wearing a skull headdress. Drescher recolored the figure for an exhibition of his paintings; before selling the piece, he scanned it, hoping that he could reuse it in a future job. A few weeks later, he was commissioned by Michelle Chu at U.S. News and World Report to supply a picture of "personal hell."

LYLE LOVETT digital creator LANCE JACKSON client SAN FRANCISCO EXAMINER MAGAZINE software ADOBE PHOTOSHOP purpose EDITORIAL
Lance Jackson composed this colorful portrait of musician Lyle Lovett for the San Francisco Examiner Magazine. Playing off his oversized celebrity status as hallmarked by his signature hair, Jackson's portrayal still reminds the viewer of the musician's quiet, quirky demeanor and inward focus by depicting him with folded hands. Shifts in complementary color paint a vivid picture of the range of emotions in Lovett's music.

TOM WAITS digital creator LANCE JACKSON client VH1 GALLERY software ADOBE PHOTOSHOP, METACREATIONS PAINTER purpose GALLERY ILLUSTRATION
from Gallery show of portraits of musicians Musician Tom Waits has waited 30 years to be recognized, but he still assumes the posture of the outcast. Illustrator Lance Jackson painted him in the role of the noble loser for a gallery show of VH1 portraits of musicians. The gesture Jackson captures is typical of Waits, whose music is a somewhat of a happily twisted, drunken stream of consciousness. The musician's appearance is disheveled: He could be Roy Orbison after shock therapy, says Jackson, or some traveling show performer, lost in America.

ENCEPHALITIS SCARE digital creator **KATHERINE STREETER** client **SALON MAGAZINE** software **ADOBE PHOTOSHOP** purpose **EDITORIAL**

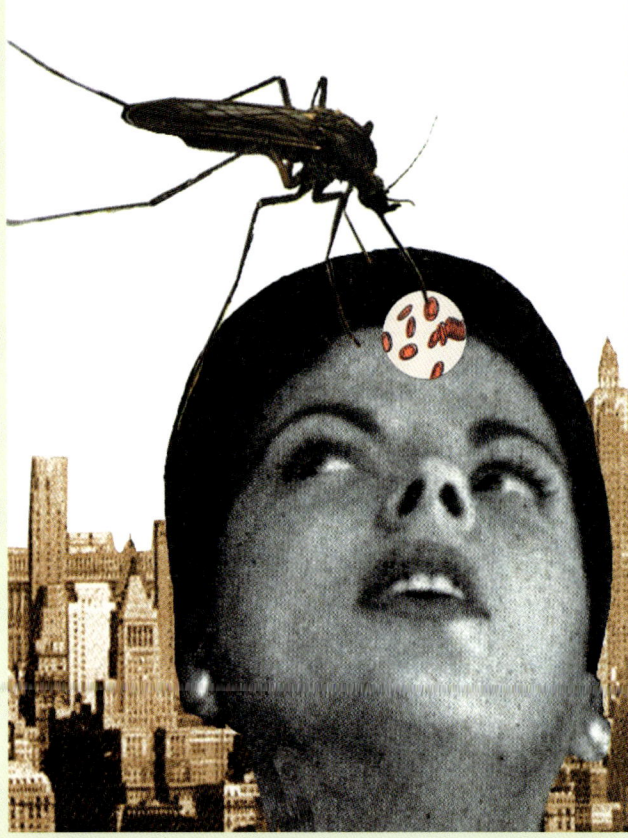

When you think about it concretely, there are few diseases more frightening than encephalitis. Born by mosquitoes, suffers can be inflicted at any time, anywhere, even in their sleep. Salon magazine, an online publication, commissioned Katherine Streeter to illustrate an encephalitis scare. The artist played up the paranoia by placing a giant mosquito on the woman's head, shooting toxins directly into the inflicted organ, the brain.

LOCKED KNOWLEDGE digital creator **KATHERINE STREETER** client **MIX MAGAZINE** software **ADOBE PHOTOSHOP** purpose **EDITORIAL**

It's a feeling every computer user knows well: Why is it so hard to get the information we need to get our machines to perform flawlessly? Why is this secret cache of knowledge guarded so carefully by the disgruntled tech support workers? Artist Katherine Streeter made this collage illustration for Mix Magazine on just that topic. Her figures are smug in their possession of what we need. She used simple blocks of color to keep it unsympathetically one-dimensional.

OFFICE GOTHIC digital creator **TOM NICK COCOTOS** client **WINDOWS NT MAGAZINE** software **ADOBE PHOTOSHOP** purpose **EDITORIAL**

Tom Nick Cocotos created this work for Windows NT magazine to accompany a story on Server Farms, an internet tool. Using a humorous play on the term "server farms", Cocotos evokes the familiar couple from the famous painting "American Gothic," placing them in an office environment. The artist's goal was not only to make a provocative illustration, but also to symbolize how simple the tool can be.